Peter and Polly Make Faces

Dominie Press, Inc.

**Polly Pig draws a circle.
Peter Pig draws a circle.**

**Polly Pig draws a big mouth.
Peter Pig draws a big mouth.**

"My mouth is sad," says Polly Pig.

"My mouth is sad,"
says Peter Pig.

They turn the faces upside down.

"Now my mouth is happy,"
says Polly Pig.
"Now my mouth is happy,"
says Peter Pig.

"A smile is a frown turned upside down."